This Coloring Book Belongs to:

MINDFULNESS

MINDFULNESS

MINDFULNESS

MINDFULNESS

MINDFULNESS

MINDFULNESS

MINDFULNESS

MINDFULNESS

MINDFULNESS

MINDFULNESS

Are you enjoying your journey into the colorful world of Lotus Blooms?

We'd love to hear your thoughts! Your experience can help others to unlock their creativity. If you could take a moment to leave a review, we would greatly appreciate it.

Use your device's camera to scan the QR code below:

Share the joy, share your thoughts, and let's color the world together!

MINDFULNESS

MINDFULNESS

MINDFULNESS

MINDFULNESS

MINDFULNESS

MINDFULNESS

MINDFULNESS

MINDFULNESS

MINDFULNESS

MINDFULNESS

MINDFULNESS

Pampered Pen is a one-stop shop for all your puzzle book needs! Whether you're a kid or an adult, we've got something for everyone. Our fun puzzle books will keep your brain sharp and your hands busy.

Our activity books are perfect for families to do together or to keep the kids entertained on a rainy day. We've got a wide variety of word search books, perfect for killing time on a long car ride or for a cozy night in.

And for the coloring book lovers, we've got a beautiful selection of coloring books for both kids and adults.

With our wide variety of puzzle books, there's something for everyone. Our themed activity books are also great for bonding with family and friends and encouraging kids to tap into their creativity.

So come check us out and treat yourself or a loved one to one of our pampering puzzle books today.

https://www.amazon.com/author/pam_pem

THANK YOU FOR YOUR PURCHASE

IF YOU ENJOYED THIS BOOK,
PLEASE CONSIDER DROPPING US A REVIEW.

IT TAKES 5 SECONDS AND HELPS
SMALL BUSINESSES LIKE OURS.

USE YOUR DEVICE'S CAMERA TO
SCAN THE QR CODE BELOW.

www.ingramcontent.com/pod-product-compliance
Lightning Source LLC
Chambersburg PA
CBHW080817280726
48660CB00018B/3489